A Poetical Offering

by Bruce Toien

A Poetical Offering
© 2020 by Bruce Toien
First Edition

This book is a work of fiction. The characters, incidents, and dialogue are drawn from the author's imagination and are not to be construed as real. Any resemblance to actual events or persons, living or dead, is entirely coincidental.

All rights reserved. No part of this publication may be reproduced, stored in, or introduced into a retrieval system, or transmitted in any form, or by any means (electronic, mechanical, photocopying, recording, or otherwise) without the prior written permission of the author, except in the case of brief quotations or sample images embedded in critical articles or reviews.

Paperback ISBN: 978-1-945587-54-2
E-book ISBN: 978-1-945587-55-9
Library of Congress Control Number: 2020910983
Bruce Toien
A Poetical Offering
1. Poetry; 2. Social Justice; 3. Relationships; 4. Passions; 5. Reflection

Book design: Dancing Moon Press
Cover design: Dancing Moon Press
Cover Art: Bruce Toien
Manufactured in the United States of America
Dancing Moon Press
www.dancingmoonpress.com

To my dear wife, my partner in life, Gail.

Contents

Introduction	7
Reflection	9
Catching Time	10
Others' Eyes	12
Many and Few	13
In the Realm of the Senses	14
Epitaph	16
Comings and Goings	17
Counsel	19
Snagging the Skin	21
The Choice in a Minute	22
Choose Your Line	23
Just For Fun	25
My Desk in Disarray	27
Lie Down with Me, Lady	28
Reflections on Tautologies	30
Family of Felines	31
Memories	33
Our Long-Ago Durham Summer	34
PÅ Norsk Og Engelsk	37
Lutefisk Blues	39
Lys i Norden (Light in the North)	41
Passions	45
Holey Tights	46
The Hand that Cracks the Glass	47
When I See Your Lips (Into the Abyss)	48
Social Justice	49
Ode to Obama, to America, to US	50
Occupation	51
A Thousand Hands	53
The Stone in the Stream	54
Relationships	55
Wild Oats	56
The Cat	57
You Are My Home	60
The Lamp	62

INTRODUCTION

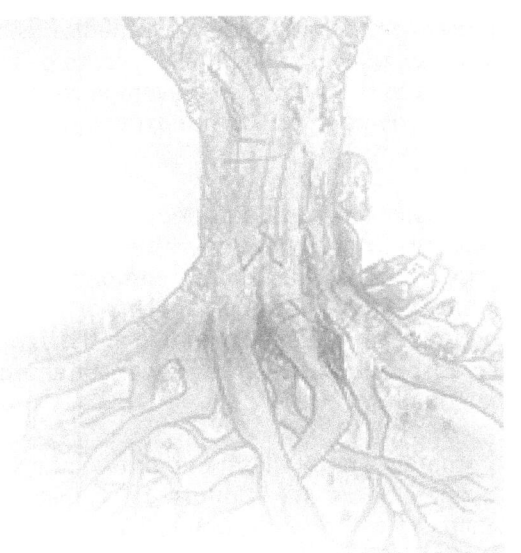

INTRODUCTION

Before you is a collection of poetry I have written over the past few decades. My output may seem meager for such a span of time. But there is a reason for that. I tend to spend weeks or even months on a single poem, setting it aside to think about it for a while, returning to tinker with it, then concluding that I'm still dissatisfied with a certain word or the rhythm of a line and setting the piece aside again to cogitate on how to solve that sticking point. And so it goes.

But "perfection is the enemy of good enough," so it's high time to share my poetry with you!

That said, I hope you'll read a poem more than once before moving on — especially the shorter, more compact ones. Also, these poems are designed to be read aloud (maybe to a friend or loved one!), so you can hear the word sounds, rhythms, alliterations and rhymes.

In that spirit, I have added commentaries after each poem to let you know what I was trying to achieve, to elucidate allusions and give context to the writing of a given piece. This is aimed at facilitating your enjoyment, as I do not expect you to do an in-depth study of each poem!

I will make a parenthetical note here: There is a tendency to believe that an author or poet is writing autobiographical revelations about her or himself. That is rarely completely true. In here, there are some descriptions of personal experience, but most of the poems are made universal by blending in the experiences of others. So it's a crapshoot whether a particular statement or poem is about me personally.

Ultimately, I hope that if one or two of my poems strike your fancy, resonate or provide comfort, you can come back to them again and again like old friends. Above all, and below all, I hope you enjoy my poetical offering to you!

REFLECTION

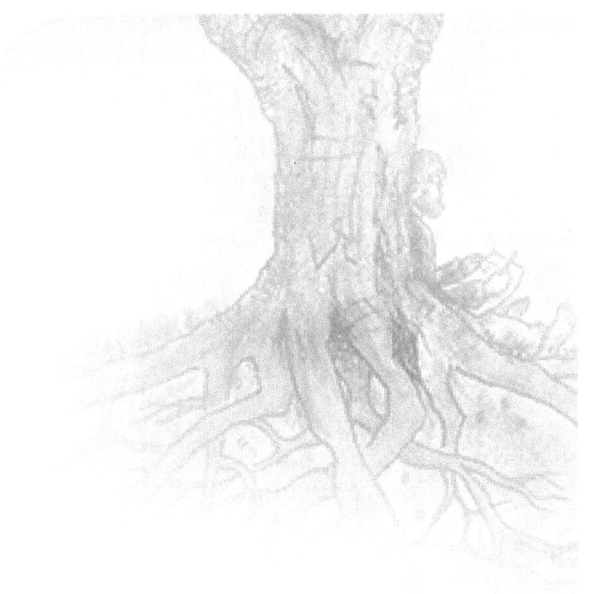

Catching Time

I'm running to catch time, time as it flees;
Oh TIME, take your time to catch me!

Don Juan the Yaqui shaman said,
"Live each day like there's no more ahead" –
    So I'm running to catch time, time as it flees;

"But lounge in the now, like life never ends!"
He winked with a smile and nodded his head —
    Oh TIME, take your time to catch me.

When first I awoke to a wondrous world,
Dazzled by possibilities, I began
    Running to catch time, time as it flees.

Was I greedy to grab for it all —
Or ungrateful the times I said no?
    Oh TIME, take your time to catch me!

Gathering the world up in my arms,
Grasping at treasures that drop from view
As I pluck up the new —
    I'm running to catch time, time as it flees;

Will I ever read Cervantes, see Kathmandu?
Sail the seas of the Southern Cross...
Nurture your dreams too?
    Oh TIME, take your time to catch me!

But holding is frantic, and I'm
Wasting wonders with warrantless worry.
For life lives in the timeless moment,
Without frenzy or hurry.

And yet and yet...

I'm running to catch time, time as it flees;

REFLECTION

Oh TIME, take your time to catch me!
Oh TIME, take your time to catch me!
Oh TIME, take your time to catch —

Commentary: This poem might well be my anthem – and maybe yours too? There is so much to experience and discover in life. Alas, our lives are too short to take it all in. Shall we race to embrace it all – or relax to savor what we have? I constructed this as a variation on the villanelle style (an example of which is Dylan Thomas' "Do Not Go Gentle into that Good Night"), repeating each of the first two lines one at a time throughout the rest of the poem until they reunite at the finale!

REFLECTION

Others' Eyes

Who am I without the mirror of others' eyes?
But what am I if I am a reflection only?
And who are you –
If you will not from time to time
See the view
Through my eyes too?

Commentary: This is my rebuttal to people who say "I don't care what anyone thinks!" All of us, except perhaps for sociopaths, care about people's perceptions of us. The opinions of important people in our lives certainly affect us and, to a greater or lesser extent, shape our identity. Likewise, your opinions of others may well affect them in a reciprocal manner.

Many and Few

We grant greatest value to
The things that are few:
Gold more than tin
Pine less than yew.

Youth squanders its hours
Because they are many.
Rueful age grasps at them so hard
They vanish through the fingers
As staring at a dim star
Disappears it from view.

As with things, we value people less
when they are many.
Yet each of us is a universe
No less for all the company.

Commentary: Do we value things and people for their uniqueness – or for themselves inherently?

In the Realm of the Senses

In the realm of the senses
How can there be
A richer reality
Than the realm of the senses?

Poetry's but a bloodless
Travesty
Of the reality of
Unushered experience.

The best it can do
Is bring the mind to
Memories from
Childhood's impressions:

The poignant comfort
Of leafy greens,
The mystery of
Translucent reds,

The quest to caper
On billowy clouds
Against infinite
Depths of indigo sky ...

Or the fragrances of
First love flowering,
The walks in lamplit
Lanes.

The here and the now
Can only be felt –
Not captured in the bell jar
Of the verbal hemisphere.

A self-annihilating
Statement this may be;
A poem striving beyond poetry
As Herbert or Thomas tried.

But thinking about thinking

REFLECTION

Talking about talking,
Cannot match
Being about being.

Commentary: Here I ponder the less than perfect ability of words to fully convey one's personal experience of the senses – the tastes and smells, sights and sounds and textures of real life. Many poets over the ages have eschewed literary finery in favor of unadorned descriptions of living, breathing, flesh-and-blood experience.

For example, there was George Herbert in the 1600s, with his "The Altar," in which he actually shapes the lines of the poem to look like an altar!

And Heinrich Heine in the 1800s, with his "Die Sassen und Tranken am Teetisch" ("They Sat and Drank at the Tea Table") in which he contrasts the refined aesthetics of the snooty elite to the earthy love making of him and his girlfriend.

And Dylan Thomas in the 1900s, with his "In My Craft or Sullen Art," in which he declares he is writing this love poem not for the fancy aesthetes but "for the lovers who lie abed" who, ironically, are not the type of people who would ever read his poetry!

Epitaph

Don't shy away!
I have something to say:
Like you, I wanted to live
I loved and cried, was bedazzled with colors and scents,
Laughed and fought, danced and dreamed.
I did not choose, nor wish to come here,
Nor, do I think, did these others whom I may or may not have known.
Like you, this somber place filled me with fear.
So I say to you now, don't be afraid, it's okay –
But don't waste your time on earth
With petty, stickling strife or fog of routine;
Shake yourself awake and drink in life each day,
Find comfort in all things, sleep restfully, play zestfully,
Feel and share life's pleasures – even pain says you're alive –
Unleash your love (you may not get a second chance)
And remember: we may be frozen lumps now, but if we could,
Oh, if only we could, we'd all dance in the sun again.

Commentary: Walking by a cemetery one day, it occurred to me that the people interred there were once alive and afraid of cemeteries themselves. So why be afraid of them?

Comings and Goings

My boots are squeezing the leaves
   into the soil
   into the reaching roots
      sucking moist earth
      up toward the sun
         for a hot transformation —
         Energy into Form:

Hard little buds are
   pushing out leaves,
   soft little leaves,
      green little ears unfolding —
      count them, one two three,
         proliferating
         where once were none
            ... just branches.

The green leaves flicker a season in the sun,
   then turn colors, one by one,
   dropping earthward, root-bound,
      soon mottled with mold —
      pullulating speckles and freckles —
         count them, one two three,
         mutually merging
            into gray-brown
            leaf-mantle.

In time, rapacious rootlets, reaching, ramifying
   find our pallid leaves.
   Now three trees suckle them,
      feeding fresh shoots —
      Radical change is surely upon them ...
         Where did they come from? (Were they ever gone?)
         Where do they go to? (Do they really go?)

Commentary: The cycle of life and death.

COUNSEL

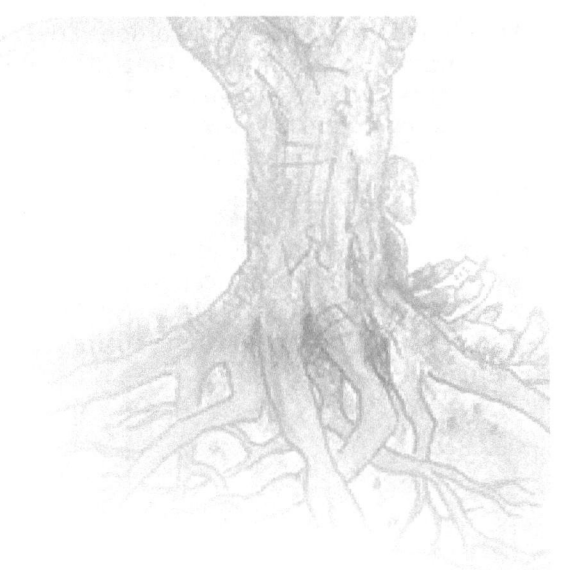

Section Preface

These poems came out of a period when I was in therapy to get relief from an anxiety disorder called obsessive-compulsive disorder (OCD). (The cognitive-behavioral therapy worked, by the way!) In contrast to the popular stereotype of OCD as a comical concern for neatness or cleanliness, such behaviors are merely a means to quell the overwhelming anxiety that is at the core of OCD: namely, painfully distressing thoughts that won't let go, no matter how obviously irrational they may be. Ironically, I've always been rather fearless about physical danger, but helpless before imagined horrors.

The most effective antidote is akin to the art of meditation (and take note: it is equally applicable to garden variety anxious thoughts that grab at most of us from time to time). The goal is learning to tolerate the thoughts, recognize them as nothing but thoughts, to welcome them in and let them drift away. But trying to "do" something about a distressing thought is what digs it in. That's what this first poem is about.

Poetry strives to lift specific personal experiences to the level of the universal so that any reader can find something in it that applies to her- or himself. In that spirit, I hope you'll find something here that can be of use to you if and when you are plagued with anxiety about something.

Snagging the Skin

It's not the thought
That snags the skin
But the fight to make it "right"
That drives it in.

By far the better way
Is let it have its say,
Then gently turn back to...
The things you meant to do.

Commentary: When faced with distressing thoughts, neither fight nor flight will help; but meditative non-resistance as the "middle way" that drains the thoughts of their power. Imagine a growling dog: the best policy is to neither challenge it nor flee but to calmly stay put until it tires of trying to scare you.

The Choice in a Minute

Each minute spent dreading and dodging distress
Is a living minute laid to rest;
But holding discomfort a mere minute longer
Is a full-measured minute of getting stronger.

Commentary: When faced with distressing thoughts, it's a waste of time and life to grapple with them. Tolerating anxiety takes its power away if you hang in there a while. Like the growling dog, anxiety will escalate initially but then become fatigued if you don't respond to it.

Choose Your Line

Choose out your line,
Pay worry no mind,
You can let it whine –
And you'll be fine.

Commentary: This is derived from my cycling experience. When flying down a steep hill and there is a curve ahead, I dispel my anxiety by saying to it, "You say I'm going to crash? Yep, that's right, I'm gonna crash! Gonna totally wipe out! And you what? That's OK with me. Ha ha, I don't care!" I can almost see the face of anxiety droop with disappointment at its failure to scare me. Meanwhile, that frees up my mind to commit full attention to slowing a bit and holding my downhill line around the curve.

JUST FOR FUN

Section Preface

The title of this section comes from one of Simon & Garfunkel's early songs, "Feelin' Groovy," which Paul Simon tagged in the lyrics printed on the back cover of the album as "just for fun" – to offer it as a light-hearted relief from the deeper and more serious other songs on the album.

My Desk in Disarray

My desk is just a freakin' mess
The heaps of clutter grow apace;
Itself no sin, you must confess –
It's just I need more space!

Why keep this potpourri?
Because (I've got to say!)
The need is guaranteed
Once I throw a thing away.

Commentary: I think this one is self-explanatory!

Lie Down with Me, Lady

What else do we need in this compressurized world!?
Oh lie down with me lady
While summer grows green
Look up at the sun skying highward;

In the greeny grass, I draw you ever nighward,
So we one and the other
Should not doubt
That the best is ever now.

Moments past and worlds yet unborn
Are not ours now, nor ever will be.
No world is more strengthy
Than the fiery front edge
Of who we are now and have ever been.

Take my hand, lady, in this danceworthy time
And rejoice in
The inwinding moment,
The indwelling spark of
The fiery front edge
Of who we are now and have ever been,
In the languid heat with
Bees humming down drowsily.

Never was king given nor queen begifted such richliness:
Insects humming down languidly
In the sleepy warmth of our twining enlovement.
Let me drop dreamily into your wine dark eyes;

Let us reawaken together to a purple evening drawing nighward,
Enfragranced with the sweetest breath of sage
From off the far radiant warm hills,
With summer's Arcturus rising brightly and ruddily
In the fiery front edge of the nighward drawing darkness
And the secret sounds of nighttime
Urging us onward.

And so soft visions issue from your soft lips speaking,
Wording me willingly into your world.

And so am I by you
Unendingly enraptured!

Commentary: This one was for the sheer fun of playing with language. It's tongue-twisting, full of quirky phrasing and invented words, much in the spirit of Dylan Thomas. Try reading it aloud ... it's a hoot!

Reflections on Tautologies

In slumber we walk
  as we walk in our sleep;
'Neath deep blue skies,
  sky-blue and deep.

We look at each other
  as our eyes now meet:
I gaze at you and
  you gaze at me.

Conversing we talk,
  we both, we two;
You speak at me
  and I speak at you.

So when we part,
  and each other leave,
We're left but sleep-dreams
  Mine of you, and yours of me.

Commentary: A tautology is a self-referencing statement that provides no additional information. For instance, I saw a humorous t-shirt that said, "All tautologies are tautologies," which is of course itself a tautology!

Here, in each stanza, the second line of each couplet restates the first, thus adding no additional information. Ultimately, the two people relate as a pair of tautologies, offering no additional information about themselves to each other before they depart.

Family of Felines

From winter's Himalayas
to the warm Western Ghats,
I'm the one known as Prakash
the princeling of cats.

I've known and loved a myriad,
but I'll speak of just a few:
The ones most dear to me
I will share now with you.

The blue-eyed was dangerous,
Allied with the night;
The next was more genial
And gentle, and white.

Another was calico,
orange, black & dun
With a toy in each corner
and a mouse on the run.

Siamese accompanied me
When we stepped onto the mall
Along the reflecting pools
Of the Taj Mahal.

There were many dear others,
Too many to say, you see.
And though I was prince of them all
It is they who ruled me.

Commentary: I wrote this one for a Thanksgiving family get-together. In it, I embedded the various surnames in my immediate family: Toien, Katz, Winters, Themal, Stept and White.

Some are easy to spot; for others, it's helpful to read the poem aloud to hear the names. Can you find them all?

Incidentally, "The blue-eyed was dangerous / Allied with the night" refers to my uncle Larry who was the only one in the family besides me with blue eyes and was a narc who was a war hero who loved to go into dangerous situations to find drug smugglers. After he died, my aunt married a gentle fellow named Jack White, hence the couplet, "The next was more genial / And gentle, and white."

MEMORIES

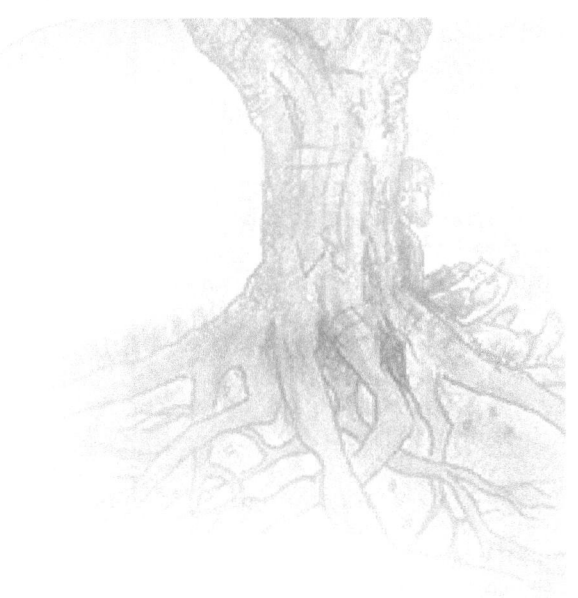

Our Long-Ago Durham Summer
(Carla, Robbin and myself in England for our high school study abroad program summer 1970)

Oh we were young then, in Northumberland,
Before everything else happened;
Before all the hardships and recoveries,
We flung ourselves fresh at life,

Saw the world through the artist's eye:
The castle keep where girls could sleep,
Away from boys like me on Old Bailey,
Planning my next rendezvous with you two.

And the cathedral, old as Hastings,
Its stonework looming under sullen skies
Above the bending River Wear,
Fired our fantasies.

The ancient was for us
Exotic, romantic and new,
We three bohemians lurking
Amongst the cleaner cut of our crew.

The mealtimes daily in the Great Hall,
With black crumbs peppering down
From frayed antique flags high on the walls
... Into my oxtail soup.

On still-hungry forays into town, I wondered
At coal-sooty miners in the Wimpy bar
And the warty brow of the gentle
Fish-and-chips monger in the square;

Oh life was an open book then
Before we read the pages.
Meeting old bowlers on the green
As we alighted from a wider world which
Those plaid-capped gentlemen
Had never seen.

And croquet on the midnight lawn – under a
Slow-dying sundown, soaked blood red;

And the pastoral green of Geordie land,
And the castle walls enlivened by
Our trysts and schemes –
Our insecurity-fueled derring-do,

We wild ones who skirted window sills
Scared and thrilled,
Sought secret passages
And lop-legged ghosts. Did others even notice our antics,
(So long ago now!)
Our headlong spree,
We unruly three?

Commentary: In the summer of 1970, having just graduated high school, I signed up with a student travel program to live for a month in Durham, England (the university town just south of Newcastle), taking classes and for the first time experiencing life in another country. Together with two new friends on the same program, Carla (who wore vampire teeth and declared herself a witch!) and her friend Robbin, we ran around the ancient town in our free time, having all kinds of adventures!

PÅ NORSK OG ENGELSK
(IN NORWEGIAN AND ENGLISH)

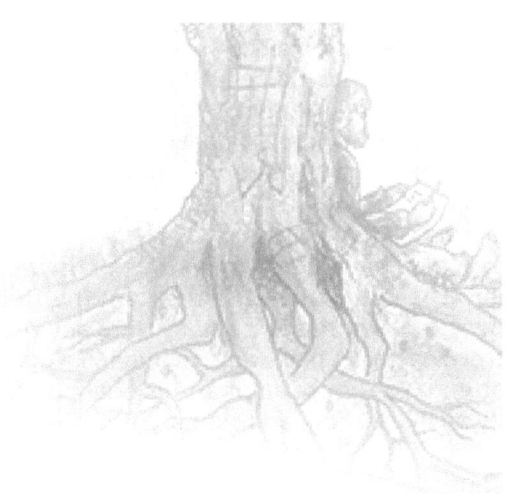

Section Preface

For decades, I've been an avid cross-country (or Nordic) skier. Norway is the cradle of that sport, so a lot of the coaching advice columns and coaches themselves come from that country. Then I found another connection: I did an internet search on my name, Toien, which my Lithuanian Jewish grandfather said was mysterious in origin and, lo and behold, I discovered that that name or its variant, Tøien, is common in Norway. Wow! I made contact with a "cousin" in Oslo and she began teaching me the Norwegian language called bokmål, which I became an ardent student of. And then I met Liv Arnesen, the Norwegian woman who was the first woman in history to ski to the South Pole. I also met her friend, Ann Bancroft, who was the first woman in history to reach the North Pole. Together, in 2001, they made history again by ski trekking all the way across Antarctica. My meeting with them was in 2003, at Powell's bookstore in downtown Portland, where they were signing their book about that trans-Antarctic adventure. I learned that the two would be leading a primarily Norwegian "ekspedisjon" across the Spitsbergen ice cap, just 600 miles from the North Pole, in 2004. Adventure skiing, Norwegian language, wow! I signed up immediately and thereupon redoubled my study of Norwegian.

During that amazing two-week trek, pulling our own 70 lb sleds, I scribbled out a poem to my wife in Norwegian first, then translated into English, about how important this trek was and it was not because I wanted to be away from her. A year after the trek, the trekking group planned a reunion in Norway which I could not attend. So I wrote a humorous poem (in Norwegian) accompanied by an illustration, and sent it off for their amusement.

Those two poems follow here.

Lutefisk Blues

På norsk
In translation

Til hele Newton-laget... om mat-valget! BT

LUTTEFISK BLUES

Vennligst ikke spis meg!
Jeg vil ikke spises, jeg ...
Bacalao smaker sannelig bedre
Og prepares mye lettre!

Men istedenfor å bruke torsk
(Som alltid gjør meg morsk!)
Kan man legge dertil tofu
I skogshytta under furu.

Nå, derfor: skjønt det ikke er
  Så veldig ekte norsk,
Vil jeg gjerne anbefale her
  Kjempevelsmakende "toforsk"!!

Oh please don't eat me!
I'd rather not be eaten, you see.
Bacalao is much tastier fare
And it's so much easier to prepare!

So instead of using codfish
(which makes me really pissed!)
You can make a tofu dish
In your cabin in the wilder-nish.

Although it's not, of course,
Authentically Norse,
May I recommend super-delish
Yummy yummy tofu-fish!

Commentary:

I did this cartoon and lyrics for my Norwegian expedition-mates, who were up in a cabin in the woods celebrating the first anniversary of our 2 week "Mount Newton Expedition" trek across Svalbard in the high Arctic. I knew they would be serving Norway's national dish, lutefisk, so this poem is a way of teasing them about that.

First, a little background:

1) The Norwegian word for cod is "torsk".
2) Codfish ("torsk") which has been soaked in lye is known as lutefisk ("lye-fish"). Lutefisk is Norway's national dish. It is to Norwegians what the hamburger is to Americans.
3) The Norwegian word for lute is "lutte" ... so here is the story of a lute-playing fish who

PÅ NORSK OG ENGELSK

doesn't want to become a "Lutefisk"!

"Hilarity ensues..."

Lys i Norden (Light in the North)

av Bruce Toien

april 2004

på Svalbard

(Til alle som blir igjen mens vi drar til klodens yttreste områder ...)

Å . . . sol der sør på himmelen,
Tenk ikke, aldri,
At jeg drar mot nord for å flykte
Fra deg.

Nei, mens jeg drar mot nord
Over is, snø, stein,
Varmer du ryggen
Og lyser opp veien min
Foran.

Og når jeg kommer inn i tåkeheimen
Gjennom frostrøyke og kulde,
Og ditt en gang så lyse ansikt
Ligger nå lavt og blekt ved horisonten
Og strålene dine har blitt svake,
Så kikker jeg over skulderen
For å forsikere meg om du er der
Ennå.

by Bruce Toien

April 2004

on Spitsbergen Island

(To all those who remain behind as we set out for the most remote regions of the globe ...)

Oh, sun in the southern sky,
Do not think, do not ever think,
That I head north to flee
From you.

No, as I trek north
Across ice, snow, rock,
You warm my back
And light the way
Before me.

And when I enter the realm of fog
And come through the frost-fog and cold,
And your once bright countenance
Lies low and pale on the horizon
And your rays have grown weak,
It's then I look over my shoulder
To assure myself that you are there
Still.

I arktiske stillheten, kryper du inn i Tankene mine ... Still, hemmelig, kattaktig. Da tenker jeg på livet vårt Der sør, hvor vi bor sammen i varmen ... Og smiler.	In the Arctic stillness, you creep into My thoughts .... Quietly, secretly, cat-like. Then I think of our life There in the south, where we live together in the warmth ... And smile.
Jeg husker du spurte meg, Tårene i øyene, Trist og fortvilet, "Hvorfor dette? Hvorfor må du reise bort? Hvorfor det?"	I remember that you asked me, Tears in your eyes, Sad, anguished and desperate, "Why this? Why must you travel away? Why?"
Derfor vil jeg prøve å forklare dette Og så håper jeg At du også vil prøve Å forstår meg, Mine følelser.	So I will try to explain, And I hope that you Will likewise try To understand me And my feelings.
Jeg reiser til nordlige områder I søk etter en del Av sjelen min, For å bli hel, – Å bli MEG – Igjen.	I set out for northern regions In search of a part Of my soul, To become whole – To become ME – Again.
Å bli den mannen Du elsker.	TO BECOME, TO REMAIN, THE MAN YOU LOVE.

Derfor må du aldri tenke,
ALDRI,
At jeg ikke behøver deg,
Ikke trenger deg,
Ikke elsker deg:
Nei, nei, for det gjør jeg jo,
Alltid.
Du er etter alt en del av sjelen min også,
Kjæreste.

Therefore you must never think
NEVER,
That I do not need you,
Do not require you,
Do not love you.
No, no, because that I do,
Always.
You are after all, a part of my soul too,
My dearest.

Commentary: Written in 2004 during my two-week trek across the Svalbard ice cap with a group of 19 adventurers — sixteen Norwegians (including trek leader Liv Arnesen, the first woman to ski solo to the South Pole), one Austrian and two Americans (myself and Ann Bancroft, the first woman to cross Greenland and to ski to the North Pole). Note: together, Liv and Ann were the first women to ski across Antarctica in 2001. Since this poem was addressed to my wife, who does not speak Norwegian, I translated it into English before presenting it to her!

PASSIONS

Holey Tights

Her holey tights were a holy fright
I just couldn't take her anywhere;
Her mouth was loud but her eyes were bright
And I loved her more than I could bear.

Commentary: Ah, High School infatuations! This is one that never happened. To me, at least!

The Hand that Cracks the Glass

I'm the hand that caresses your face ...
And the bunched fist that cracks the glass.

I'm the bended arm under the dancer's swoon ...
And the sharpened elbow that clears the room.

I'm the palm that shelters love in clasp,
Then drops it for what it cannot grasp.

I'm the face that feels your caress ...
Then sees itself in the hand-cracked glass.

Commentary: This is one of my darker pieces. Each couplet focuses on the way any part of ourselves has agency for love or hatred, comfort or violence. More generally it's a reflection on how all of our abilities, skills, talents, knowledge can be enlisted to promote good or ill.

When I See Your Lips (Into the Abyss)

When I see your lips so full and moist
I feel my mouth kissing them gently,
Touching them tenderly,
Skimming them, oh so lightly.
It's then a wave of such desire wells inside me,
So strong and so sweet
That I feel I will weep.
And just when I fear I will draw you
Impulsively into my arms,
Dropping the talking jaws
Of those in our party ...
The delicious madness subsides, just a bit;
Eases away from my shore, just a little;
And with it, my dilemma.

My senses regained,
I clutch at the cords of continuing conversation,
Subdue my quickened breathing.
And smile vacantly.

But I know that soon, that dark, wine-dark surge
Will sweep in over me again,
Drenching me in achingly sweet ecstasy.
And my strong limbs
Will grow uncharacteristically weak
And begin trembling.
Then, with the tide swinging me full around on my mooring,
I'll wonder if I can yet hold on.
Because I long, oh how I long!
To let go.
And drown
In you
Completely.

Commentary: The darkness that looms beyond helpless, headlong desire.

SOCIAL JUSTICE

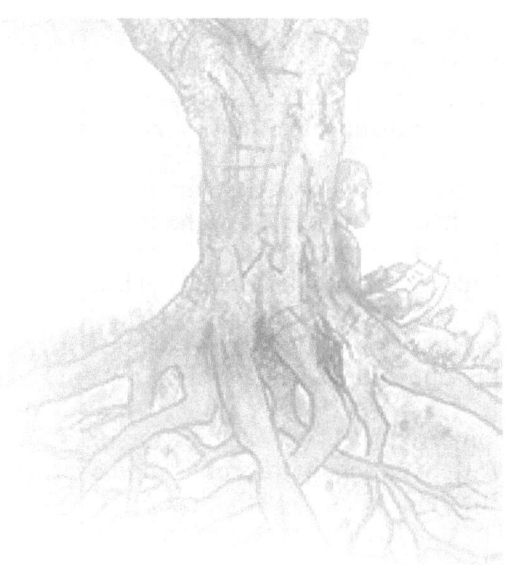

Ode to Obama, to America, to US
On the occasion of Barack Obama's election on November 4, 2008 as the 44th President of the United States

Some have called our collective reaction
To this historic moment, "joyous disbelief",
But slumped out on our sofa, in tears,
Exhaling sighs, I just call it dazed relief.

After our long national trauma,
This native son of ours, this Obama,
Has voiced our longings, invited us to sing
An old dream and a new world into being.

But this is not the end says Barack,
For the hard work's just begun.
No finish line, as they say, for there is none
In our questing, in our life's race run.

Or swum. Where buoyed an instant above the waves
We glimpse with our own happy eyes
There is indeed a shore out there to gain
And for now that knowledge will suffice.

For this is our moment, the window is cracked,
The door stands ajar, we've found our track.

Tomorrow we'll yet again be tasked
With daunting matters of life and death.
But today at least, with rancor past,
I'm glad to simply catch my breath!

Commentary: I have a photograph from 2008 of my wife, Gail, and I sitting on our sofa with little American flags in our hands and tears welling in our eyes after it was announced that Barack Obama had won the presidency. It felt like a breaking dawn. Alas, that day has been followed by grim nightfall.

Occupation

A linking of arms

Against the brusque rush
Of hooves and batons
Beating on black Lexan shields

Meant for defense ...
Against defenselessness.

We fall back
But the line holds,
Face to visored face
Against helmeted brothers and sisters
Black clad in the night,

Servants of order ...
Some eager, some heartbroken.

(It's not you, but the machine we're fighting!)

We are the grass under old asphalt,
Growing through sunlit cracks
Crazing the lifeless black
Asphalt.

We are tender green vines
Twining up through
Imposing dead towers
Of steel and glass,

Ozymandias monuments to mad avarice:
Rapturous, seductive, euphoric ...
And deadly.

Yes, a rootling can split a rock
Yes, grass can push through
The brittlest pavement.
Life will not be denied,

SOCIAL JUSTICE

As it probes
Patient and persistent ...
Reaching for the light.

Commentary: This is a blend of my own experience downtown with the Occupy movement and a friend's experience during one harrowing nighttime confrontation with the police.

A Thousand Hands

It's a thousand hands made the self-made man.

The roads he drives across the land.
His food grown by the farmer's hand,
The teachers who gave him his lesson plans.

It's a thousand hands made the self-made man.

No pity has he for those low-wage fools!
Their fault alone they missed the better schools.
So says he in his mansion on the hill
Wearing tailored finery and jewelry finer still
Surveying his factories below, continuously manned.
Well...

It's a thousand hands made the self-made man.

No excuse they started out poor, started out down,
Lived in dangerous parts of town
No excuse to live on the fringe says he with a frown,
No excuse they started off brown.

Just nose to the grindstone, and never stop
Hard work's all you need to get to the top
So says he, making his stand
But...

It's a thousand hands made the self-made man.

Commentary: The myth of the self-made man.

The Stone in the Stream
Ode to conservatism

That stone is immovable,
That's what he says: "I am immovable.
This is the right and only place to be,
Mid-stream, I'm a bulwark
Against the foolish flow."

While currents career around
And over the bed-hugging
Chert or granite or whatever he is
He is not moved.

Until the rains bloat the brook
That jostles the rock
Till he tumbles and travels
Forward a piece,
Coming to rest as he inevitably will,
And stonily declares again,
"I am immovable.
This is the right and only place to be,
Athwart the stream of events,
Restraining the restless waters
From their folly
I stand firm.

"Sure I was foolish in that place before,
But here I take a stand immovable,
For this is the right-thinking place to be.
And I will not be moved."

The stream flows on.

Commentary: *It occurred to me not long ago that most Conservatives don't necessarily want to go backwards, they just want to maintain whatever the current status quo is, even though they had to be dragged, kicking and screaming, by progressives and other social groups to this point. And they will protest against being dragged further, though eventually they will embrace that new status quo.*

RELATIONSHIPS

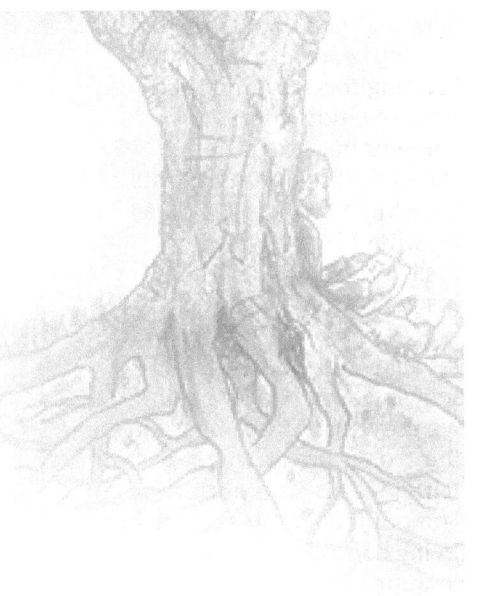

Wild Oats

Oh, we've come a long road

My mate, my love!
So much has happened,
So much has happened;
Yet in an instant I can fly back
In my mind's eye —

Back to the first green awakening times
When we two were wild rootlings
The hot sap rising in our veins,
Driving forth urgent life
Gyrating madly towards the sun
And into each other's arms;
Bending this way and that,
We knew not where,
But ever back together.
For wild young green shoots,
Growing wildly,
Are vital but fragile
Easily bruised
Easily broken.

Yet splaying and twining
Splaying and twining again,
We grew strong as one great tree.
Our trunks are now grown stout
With love and memories
And our leafy embrace has grown
So inextricably entwined,
So impossibly interbranched
That I can no longer tell
Where I end
And you begin,
My mate,
My love.

Commentary: A long love life with a wonderful wife!

The Cat

I see your body move with feline grace
And strength.
I feel your gentle warmth
And sleek fur
Draw up beside me,
Purring.

But under my stroking hand,
I sense the supple muscles
Are rippling with electricity –
Ready to bolt,
Again.

Your back arches affectionately
Under my arm,
Against my breast,
Tail tickling my chin.

And now I hear another's purring,
(Could it be mine?)
Murmuring in concert with yours.
But...

I dwell in a faraway neighborhood
And soon must be underway,
Again.

And then I will need to bid you
Sad adieu.
This must be.

With secret tears rimming my eyes,
I stroke your fur a bit too hard
This time.

And you jump away –
Startled;

RELATIONSHIPS

Catlike, canny, not to be trapped,
Nor cornered or boxed in –
Remembering perhaps
Some ancient abuse
To your wild spirit,
Untamable.

The memory of some fencing-in
That made you forever vigilant, cautious,
Even among the ones who love you...
Ever wary.

My hand sweeps now
        through empty air.
A cold pang slices
        through my full heart.

But I understand.
And wait.
It's OK.

And anyway,
I have errands to attend
And poems to write
And people I must meet today,
As usual.

Yet I cannot help but wonder
About the lonely longings
And secret hurts
Immured within your feline
Heart.

I want them to come forth,
And grow acquainted with,
and gingerly speak with
Their blood cousins who dwell
In my own...

And thus allow both
To cease their solitude
And be lonely
Never again.

But now your absence is palpable;
What can I do but let go?
It's time to move on,
And then...

After some time I feel,
I think I feel, yes I feel,
A certain special cat arching her back
Under my arm,
Against my breast,
Tail tickling my chin.
Again.

Yes, it's you, you've come back!
And now I feel you swatting
At the buttons on my shirt.
And now I cover them with my hand:
You see, I need to protect myself too,
But...

I secretly hope you will pull them off
Anyway.

For when I steal a glance into your wild eyes
Sparkling with wordless mischief.
I know that you want to play now.
Again.

And everything is wonderful,
Again.

Commentary: Feline or woman or child? I leave it to you!

You Are My Home

You are my home, though over time,
Many homes have passed my life through.
The home that is my home has no place:
You are my home. My home is you.

My memories are oh, so much richer
For the memories I've had with you,
They pull deep savor from mundane days;
As a roux, they thicken the stew.

 You are my home.

In my noisy quotidian world,
All my thoughts are shot through with thoughts of you.
They bring me comfort, calm the clamor,
And color everything I do.

 My home is you.

While sifting the deeds of the day,
Each day's reward is the time together we spend
Sharing, sparring, teasing, pleasing,
Doing, sitting book-end-to-end.

 You are my home.

Like a private place in the woods,
Lit by sunshine, soft and warm,
Your counsel is where I know I can go
When my life is shaken with storm.

 My home is you.

As in a sunny glade in the forest,
I bask in your warmth – time and again.
But as you do my moods, I know yours:
The joys and delights, the hurt, the pain.

So when the wintry wind shivers the leaves
And the cloud lies dark on your face,
I feel your chill and want to warm you —
Warm you in my ardent embrace.

Because, because, by now you must see ...
I am your home. Your home is me.

Commentary: I wrote this poem for my wife but, as poetry should, I think it says something universal about all good and loving marriages.

RELATIONSHIPS

The Lamp
**Written to accompany our gift of an oil lamp for
Aunt Diane and Uncle Bob Winter's
50th wedding anniversary
March 9, 2002**

Oil and wick
Wick and oil.

They dance their glow upon us all
While all the while their flame's warmth draws
The one ... to the other.

Wick and oil
Oil and wick.

Their warm and mellow light
Has burned so many more
Than just one or eight nights ...

But yet it's true that all the same
It's a bright white spark
That lights the flame.

Commentary: My aunt and uncle married at ages 16 and 19. There was no reason to expect the marriage would last. Just like the oil lamp in the re-dedicated temple which contained only one night's worth of oil. And yet the oil lamp miraculously lasted eight nights, giving rise to the Jewish celebration of Chanukah. And my aunt and uncle's marriage has gone far beyond the occasion of this poem: This year (2020) they will celebrate 68 years!

RELATIONSHIPS

About the Author

Bruce Toien lives with his wife in Sherwood, Oregon. Bruce recently published *The Yamhill Barber*, a well-received mystery/humor novel set in a small town in Oregon's wine country. He has written stories and poetry since adolescence and has published two prior pieces: an analysis of T.S. Eliot's poetry in the *DeKalb Literary Journal* in the late 1970s and, more recently, a novel, *The Yamhill Barber*, which he illustrated. He has bachelors degrees from the University of California in English Literature and Physics. Like his wife, Gail, Bruce is an avid outdoorsman, enjoying running, cycling and nordic skiing. In 2004 he joined a Norwegian ski trek across Spitsbergen Island near the North Pole. In the process of learning Norwegian, he wrote two poems in that language, which he later translated into English and those appear in this volume. He is currently working on a new science fiction novel based on his Spitsbergen adventure called *Signatures in the Ice*. Bruce works in IT, currently at Kaiser Permanente, as a database architect and developer.

www.ingramcontent.com/pod-product-compliance
Lightning Source LLC
Chambersburg PA
CBHW030138100526
44592CB00011B/946